All children have
a strong desire to read
to themselves...

and a sense of achievement when they can do so. The **read it yourself** *series has been devised to satisfy their desire, and to give them that sense of achievement. The series is graded for specific reading ages, using simple vocabulary and sentence structure, and the illustrations complement the text so that the words and pictures together form an integrated whole.*

LADYBIRD BOOKS, INC.
Lewiston, Maine 04240 U.S.A.
© LADYBIRD BOOKS LTD MCMLXXIX
Loughborough, Leicestershire, England

Printed in England

The Magic Paintbrush

adapted by Fran Hunia
for easy reading from the traditional tale
illustrated by Martin Aitchison

Ladybird Books

Liang was a poor boy who lived in a little town in China. He couldn't go to school, because he had to work all day. He made just enough money for the things he needed to live on.

There was one thing Liang wanted, and that was to paint. But he had no paintbrush, and not enough money to buy one.

Liang couldn't paint without a paintbrush, so he had to content himself with drawing. After work he liked to sit in the sun and draw pictures on flat stones.

He drew beautiful pictures of birds and trees and flowers. People came to look at his drawings.

"What beautiful pictures!" they all said. "They look so real!"

Liang was pleased that people liked his drawings.

As Liang was walking home from work one day, he looked in the window of a school. He saw a teacher painting a picture.

Liang went in and said to the teacher, ''I am a poor boy but I want to paint very much. Could

you give me a paintbrush, please?"

The teacher was angry.

"Go away," he said. "Painting is not for poor boys like you. Get out of my school!"

The teacher went back to his painting, and Liang walked away.

Liang went home. He ate supper, and then he went to bed. Soon he was dreaming. He dreamed that an old man was by his bed, talking to him. The old man had a golden paintbrush.

"This is for you," he said. "Take it, but be careful what you do with it. It's a magic paintbrush."

The old man put the golden
paintbrush on Liang's bed and
walked away.

The next day, as Liang was getting up to go to work, he saw a golden paintbrush on his bed. He picked it up and looked at it.

"My dream was real!" he said. "The old man *did* give me a paintbrush! Now I can paint all I want."

Liang couldn't wait to start.

First he painted a beautiful bird.

As he finished the picture, the
bird came to life. It flew up from
the picture and out the window.
Liang looked at it in amazement.

The next thing Liang painted was a little fish. As he finished the picture, the fish came to life, and Liang had to run and put it in some water.

Liang painted all day long. One after the other, his pictures came to life.

Liang didn't have to go to work after that. He could paint all the things he needed.

Soon people heard about Liang's magic pictures, and they came to see him paint. They watched in amazement as Liang's paintings came to life.

Poor people came to Liang and asked him to paint pictures of things they needed. Liang was happy to help them. He painted chairs for some old people and a horse for a poor farmer. He went on painting day after day.

Soon the emperor heard about
Liang and his magic paintings.

"I must ask that boy to come
and paint for me," he said. "He
could paint all kinds of things. I
could have all the gold I want!"

18

The emperor
ordered his men to go
and get Liang. Soon Liang came
to talk to the emperor.

"Thank you for asking me to work
for you," he said, "but I paint things
for poor people. You don't need help."

19

The emperor was angry that Liang didn't want to work for him.

"I will make you work for me!" he said.

He ordered his men to take Liang away and lock him up in the stables.

"You will be cold out there," said the emperor. "In a day or two you will do as I ask."

Liang was taken away and locked in the stables.

It was cold in the stables. Liang painted a fire. Next he painted a chair so that he could sit by the fire. Then he painted some good things to eat.

After two days the emperor said, "Liang must be so cold by now that he will be glad to come and work for me. I will go and talk to him."

The emperor went out to the stables. He looked in and saw all the things Liang had painted. He was so angry that he ran back to the palace and ordered his men to go and tie Liang up.

The emperor's men went out to the stables. They looked for Liang, but he wasn't there. He had painted a ladder and escaped!

The emperor started up the
ladder after Liang, but he was
too big, and he soon fell down.
He ordered his men to take
some horses and go after
Liang. But Liang saw them
coming. He painted a horse and
escaped again.

Now Liang was in danger. The emperor was waiting for him to go home so that he could get him and lock him up again. Liang didn't know what to do. He didn't want to keep painting magic pictures. He wanted to be a real painter.

"I know what I can do," he said. "I will keep painting, but I won't finish my pictures. Then they won't come to life."

Liang went from town to town painting pictures and selling them. He was careful not to finish his paintings, so they didn't come to life.

No one knew who Liang was,
and no one knew that his paintbrush
was magic. Liang was happy that
people liked his pictures. He was
glad to be a real painter now.

Then one day Liang painted a beautiful big bird. He was careful not to finish the picture. But as he was about to sell it, a man bumped into him. Some paint fell on the picture and finished it. The bird came to life and flew up out of the painting.

People looked at the bird in
amazement. They saw that
Liang's painting had come to life.

"This boy is magic," they said.

A man ran off to see the emperor.

"There is a painter in town who is magic," he said. "He painted a big bird that came to life and flew away."

The emperor knew that it must be Liang. He ordered his men to get Liang and lock him up again.

"Take his magic paintbrush away," said the emperor. "Then he can't paint things to help him escape."

The emperor's men locked Liang up. They took his magic paintbrush and gave it to the emperor.

"Now I will see if this magic paintbrush will work for me," said the emperor.

He painted some gold. As soon as he had finished the picture, he picked up the gold and looked at it. It was real!

"It works!" said the emperor.
"Now I can have all the gold
I want!"

He went on painting more and
more gold until it fell on top of
him. His men had to help him out
from under the gold.

After that the emperor painted gold bars. One of the gold bars was really big. When the emperor picked it up, it turned into a big snake.

The snake chased the emperor, and his men had to come and help him get away.

Now the emperor knew that he needed Liang's help to paint the things he wanted.

"I will have to talk Liang into painting for me after all," said the emperor.

He went to talk to Liang.

"Paint pictures for me, and I will let you marry the princess," he said.

Liang didn't want to marry the princess, but he didn't want the emperor to know that.

"Yes," he said. "Give me my paintbrush, and I will paint for you."

"What do you want me to paint?" asked Liang.

The emperor ordered him to paint the sea, and Liang did as he said. The sea looked beautiful.

"Now let's have some fish in the sea," said the emperor. Liang painted all kinds of fish. One by one he picked them up and put them in the sea.

"I want to go sailing," said
the emperor. "Paint me a boat."

Liang painted a beautiful boat
with big red sails. The emperor

and his men got on the boat, and
Liang waited to see what the
emperor wanted next.

"Now paint some wind so that we can sail," said the emperor.

Liang painted some wind, and the boat started to sail away. Liang painted some big waves. The boat went up and down on the waves.

"Stop painting," ordered the emperor, but Liang kept painting more and more big waves.

The boat went up and down, up and down.

"Stop, stop! I order you to stop!" said the emperor, but Liang kept painting. He painted more and more wind and waves until the ship went down under the water. Then he walked away.